Giving & Taking

Giving & Taking

a poetry collection

Kimberly Joy McBride

Published by Tablo

for Kim

Early

She wants to carve out
The apple inside her

Pluck the fruit from her tree
Rip apart its redness

Steal the seed
Swallow it

Let an ocean of acid
Render worthless
Her rebirth

Only then will she be herself

Not the satiation for
Searching eyes

Eyes that seem to steal
Before hands even touch

But soon their flesh will
Tear into hers

Ravenous climbers
Mount her trunk
Seize her leaves
Strip her bark

Her limbs will buckle under
The weight of their want

She knows that in the end
Her corpse will be used as
Kindle for their own fires

So instead, she chooses
To make bare her own branches

So instead, she chooses
To fertilize the soil of herself

Stem the flow of her lifeblood
Let her precious rubies
Drop and rot in the earth

For she has always seen the beauty
Of the trees no one touches

Roots planted so firmly
They seem one with the Earth

Finally the taker.

4

Golden Chains

She climbed to the 45th floor
of the Empire State Building
And entered the pawn broker's glass enclosure

Her fingers lifted into the light
A ziploc bag filled with gold
Cascades of chains and ropes
Interlocked like a waterfall of wealth
She could hold in her hands

The merchant counted
The worth of her former life
Twenty-four carats from Morocco
Sixteen from Spain
With Italy so soft you could mold it between your fingers

Because she would rather sell herself
Than give up the dream of him

Fouetté

What feels real to me
Are the thoughts that spin
In my mind like tiny ballerinas
Executing the controlled choreography of chaos

The worries and wants
That have been rehearsed so many times
Only a single note needs to ring
For the show to begin

Break an ankle
Break a foot
Break my body
Into these thin hard lines
If I just spin fast enough
I can break through

I only ever wanted to be
The solo dancer on the stage
Luminous within the spotlight
Which blinds me to the audience

Please marvel at my mastery

Because what is unknown
Is a partner who catches me
Or moving the way my limbs long to
Messy, soft, sensual

I cannot collapse
I did that once

The sprung floor shattered
Beneath my knees
I flew against flying
Gravity almost burying me

So I vowed never to misstep again

Therapy Notes

Her evil eyes
Scan my screen

Not in evil in the sense of wicked
But because they are the same shade
As those medallions that offer protection

I guess that's similar
To what she gives to me

But as she reads my words to my mother
I know she is thinking
How hard it must have been
To tame this volcano of a girl
Without burning yourself

Breaking the Horse

i said i don't believe in hell,
baby boy,
we're already here

god isn't dead
he's just our unconscious

he's everything inside
causing us to self-destruct

the pessimist was right
we can want what we will
but not will what we want

we say we want the light so much
why haven't we surrendered?

why hasn't jesus come down
and scooped us into salvation?

maybe he's not really here

maybe god and the devil
are the same man with two faces
of everything we can't control

it can all be so easy
but what goddess am i
within the easy?

so we rage on

screaming ourselves in defiance
of this world we came into
all illusions

hoping to break into something
like damascus
not our conversion
but the world's

write me thirteen letters, baby
can't you see i should be worshipped?

and i might sooner break myself
than break my expectations
for this purgatory of humanity

only one can survive

Unspoken

What they don't tell you
Is that there are still good times

Those are the times
That make you doubt

Those are the times
That make you stay

Chaos for the Fly

We wove webs
around each other

"Be what I need"

The delicate match
Of sticky strings

Tying knots within our
Empty spaces

Hoping to finally find
something whole

We only wounded ourselves

Sixteen arms trapped
By need

Sixteen eyes paralyzed
by projections

Until there was no room
Left to breathe

We each masqueraded
As flies

But it was a stalemate
of spiders

Yellow Bird

Let's get drunk off spicy margaritas
And fill up on free chips
Make fun of the girls with silicone lips
Even though ours would be inflated too
If we could afford it

I won't make fun of you
For going back to your ex
If you won't bring up
The fact that my closest relationship
Is with my therapist

I treat intimacy like an arcade game
And you fall in love too easily
But you remind me that it's okay to cry
And I'll kill anyone who lays a hand on you
Like he did on Halloween

We talk about past lives
That you've been gone for a while
And I got sling-shotted back too quickly
I'm too tired
And you're too dreamy
But this overpriced tequila
Makes us both laugh
Until we don't care about
What our bellies look like

Let's order churros for dessert

I hate how you date republicans

And forget to respond to my texts
But I know you get frustrated
By how I can be volatile
Like our city's brush in September

So for now we'll hold each other
As we grow in different directions

Blades

I am blades of grass
you are the mower
razors edges cutting
over and over
but I cannot make a sound

do you know how many field mice
are killed each harvest season?
gerbils and rabbits too

I thought vegetarianism would save me
I thought prayers would protect me
but my life has still suffered casualties

maybe I am one too

as you enter my body
over and over
but my "no" leaves no sound

Black Bird

A yellow bird can only fly
In a single direction
Circling
While she is afraid of her own shadow

With darkness brings depth

Why I love poetry

I grew to hide my needs
Within the cruxes of metaphor

Reflecting Pool

Our high noon has passed
And now with the water
Flat and still
I can see the deep end
For what it is

I was looking for a white whale
In a reflecting pool

And it was easy to bend the image
Into what I wanted
Until I realized
Like Narcissus
It was only my own self
Staring back

Sprint

Please show me the way
To outrun myself

To make my limbs go faster
Than my spirit

To shed that self
Until I am only movement

No more mind

Only feet pushing back pavement
Propelling across
A finish line
Where I will find
The arms of someone
Who will make me whole
Without myself

I have never wanted her
She has only been dead weight

Mon Petite Mort

The day I finally
Let myself let go

And just go

And go

Is the day I have to admit
I am a woman

And a woman doesn't wait to be saved

Letting Go

A part of you fits into
every category. Love and
hate. Friend and
enemy. Mentor and
muse. What I believe this is,
is more delicate than
a raindrop and more complex than
the fractals when winter turns her
to ice.

But I know that I have a tendency
to be foolish and naïve. That I look
a gift horse in the mouth while
it spits on me, hoping to turn
its violent tongue into treasures. That
I stay, too long, with people
who do not want me, cannot
help me, hoping to rewrite
the song of my youth,
held on an unfinished note of
longing for all these years. The only resource for my breath.

I still try with him. He tramples
me every time.

I fear it's the same with you.

The chorus of friends say
stay and go, more goes than
stays, but I hold the few sweet

s's like when I learned how to stop lisping. The crisp hope of a
better future where I am not this
ugly self anymore.
Rid me of myself. And all my shame.
All these weak patterns that cannot tell
black from white. They invert before
my eyes. I know what I want, but wanting
and needing are two different things, and you
have spread out amongst the tree
of my life at every possible wrong turn
and every right one.

Four Words

It does not matter
If you love me
What does matter is
I don't believe it

A Failed Crop

We grew a garden of beautiful tulips

One day,
While I was tending to the soil
I stumbled upon some rose seeds

I kept them hidden in my breast pocket
Not knowing if the roses would ruin
Our thriving tulips

But yesterday,
The season for sowing seemed to be
Coming to a close
And the siren song of a new bloom
Was screaming inside of me

I could no longer stay silent

So now you know
That I hold these seeds
It is up to your hands
To plant them

My Best Friend's Boyfriend

My friend just got a boyfriend
And the clock has now struck nine
On another female friendship
That I thought would be divine

They come in the same package
Tall, dark, and suavely dressed
Buying drinks and food and movies
Thinking she will be impressed

The hour turns to ten
And he first starts let it slip
When words of judgement and coercion
Start appearing from his lip

I begin to broach with caution
The warning signs I see
Making sure to talk him cheery
So she can't put blame on me

Hands point to eleven now
Worries have turned into streams
Of tears rolling down her face
As her heart pulls at its seams

"Leave him," I say "and run"
"You deserve so much more"
But she's with him, I'm locked out
Waiting, calling through the door

In a flash it's turned to midnight

And I'm crying in my bed
Once again longing for comfort
While she chooses him instead

Taffy

If there is a secret
That I want to find

It is how to wrap the moon
Around herself
Spin her until she is
Somehow
Two sides at once

It is how to stay suspended
In that breath before I wake
The warmth
Of the womb
Remembered

How do I forget about birth?
Whose anxious fingers
Of inevitable endings
Are waiting to pull me
By my neck?

How do I stretch the
Molten sugar of a
Moment
Into the candy of
Forever?

Because I cannot seem
To savor sweetness
While counting my bites

Gentle

Some things in life
Have to be done with force
But many others
Are like a glass doll
Frozen in a block of ice
Taking a hammer to it
Could destroy the prize
You might just have to wait
And allow time to work its magic

(Gently)

Maybe that is where care lies,
In the restraint

Concrete

I don't quite know
When I began to lose you
Maybe it was when "God bless you"
Stopped being my mother's nighttime prayer
Instead, that became the psalm
Of men old enough to raise me
Eyes crawling, studying my convexity
A topic I had just learned that week in geometry

I was forced to grow in a city with no meadows
Had to exist in a world where I was no longer a person
But the manifestation of a rib
And I've run 800 miles away
From everything that replaced my blood
With concrete
Trying to find something greener
But the men here still view me
As a way to lay their bricks
Creating their kingdom come

And when I say my half-empty
Hail Mary's
I wonder who I long for more
The God I loved
Or the little girl who loved him

60201

I'm having flashbacks
To Chicago

The coldness of my apartment
Drywall, glass, and stainless steel
Sharing elevators with business students
Learning how to kill our country
And looking so happy doing it

They knew how to have families,
Communities,
Wedding invitations stuck to the fridge
Little things I have now learned
Make up a life

I was always reaching for the ephemeral
More

I never found my fit

Only lonely lunch lines
And landmines of personalities
Maybe my own was the catalyst

The greatest war was waged within myself

But I miss some of it too

The snow on my windshield in Kenilworth
Peering into homes with television screens
Synchronized to the Cubs

The Midwestern dads in my office
Who cared about my life
Even when there was nothing to report

The church I abandoned
That at least held me warm
When I had no other home

Maybe I'm remembering these moments
Because I'm ready to move
Through California too

Sophomore Slump

We knew exactly which salt
To spread in each other's wounds
Which fingers to stick
In the tenderness of flesh
Twisting to the vein
Stinging

We thought our lives were zero sum

Immovable Objects

Sometimes life pushes
Until you surrender
As the punishment
For your pride

Quick
Come
Let the circus marvel
At the girl who thought
She could fly

She keeps trying
Despite the stories
Of wax wings

Hoping she won't have to humble

That she can just
Float away

Emergence

I have been reading about
What is called
"Strong Emergence"

How a hydrogen atom
Isn't wet
Neither is
A single water molecule

Yet your clothes still
Soak against your skin
After a downpour

I have been wondering
What the point of
Relationships are

Maybe the love
That emerges
Is greater than the sum of its parts

Greater than you and I

In the next life

The mural on the corner of Beverly and La Cienega
Held your face for over a year

I always wondered if the artist knew you too

The day after I left you
A Ben and Jerry's advertisement
Painted over your eyes

So I drove further East
Bought a candle
To cut our cord
Burned it until
The end of the month
When it left two small stones
One black one white

I didn't understand
Until I picked up
The Alchemist

Urim and Thummim

I tried to get them out
But they were still encased in wax

Asked the universe
For an omen

Went to my car hoping for fresh air
A stone sat on my windshield

Three sides black
One side white
"Yes."

I drove East again

Ben and Jerry were gone
Your face had returned

I screamed
Then laughed
But my throat was tight
And my chest heavy
Still feeling the need to leave

Called my friend and told her
How the universe was returning you
"Or maybe it's showing you they will always be there"

You've left me signs
Like my dead loved ones
And for that, I thank you

And maybe I'll see you
And maybe love you
Again
Even if it's only in the next life

Burning Bush

I am the art that I am looking to create

Sonnet 1 (Oxford, Summer 2016)

If I should place your hand upon my heart
And ask if you perchance would like to stay,
Could intertwining fingers never part
Even if we should travel upwards' way?
Then crawl within the place that I call home;
I invite you to full discovery.
Uncover what I keep beneath this dome
Gilded aloof with shrouded secrecy.
With your accepted hand, I show myself
And give myself destruction in your palm.
Now do I risk to lose my prided wealth
By opening the gates that rust makes calm?
    So, silence gags me to not speak my mind,
    Afraid that you will not like what you find.

Fin.

I thought endings were for everyone but me
Then I got exhausted trying to outpace
The Moon
Help the Sun keep her head above water

I am not a plane
Or a bird
I am a woman without wings
Simply having to put
One foot in front of the other
To carry me where I need to be

What a beautiful and tragic existence it is
To be human

I hoped you and I could be together
I still hope
But I must release us
So that if anything is meant to happen
It can take root on its own
Without my constant tending

Let death come when it will

I must accept that goodbyes
Are a part of every story
No matter how beautiful

And even my own iterations
Must eventually pass away

Metamorphosis

The caterpillar,
If she were to simply become
Immobile goo
Would not survive
The journey into butterfly-hood

No, she must
Harden herself first
And find her protection
Before making her inner transformation
Into disillusion

Only then does she have the strength
To release herself
From that harshness
And land wherever she wants
Free in every moment

Belief is the thing with shackles

I never realized I had a body
Until just now
This soft and heavy thing
Working as a barometer with each breath

She knows all truths
Or so they say

Somewhere deep inside me
Is a box Pandora dares not touch
For fear of the secrets
Truths too terrible to be written

I hope they are merely beliefs
That time will prove false

My new prayer

I do not know,
so let me be.
I do not know,
so let me grieve.

Acknowledgments

Mom and Dad, Aunt Kathy, Aunt Pat, Grandpa, Fred, Mandi, Max & Gracie & Audrey & Olivia, Isabel & Ivy & James, Kaja, Alica, Erica, Kate, Ali, Maddie, Emmy, Ami, Toby, Tory, Lloyd, Jacob, Courtney, Emily, Sheila, Ida, Amy, Craig's, Jim, Hanna, Jeff, Susan, Rebelle Society, Harness Magazine, Elle Leva Magazine, the greats, the goods, the not-so-greats, Mary, Audre, Patti, Marion, Taylor, Florence, Maggie, Hozier, Ella, William, Billy, Elton, New York City, Evanston, Oxford, Williamstown, Los Angeles, Ohio, the Ocean, Water (in general), the FDNY, SAG-AFTRA, Dolphins, Elephants, Giraffes, Lions, Butterflies, Roses, and Otters.

CPSIA information can be obtained
at www.ICGtesting.com
Printed in the USA
BVHW071651230821
615050BV00006B/74